Medical
Mysteries

Science Researches
Conditions from Bizarre
to Deadly

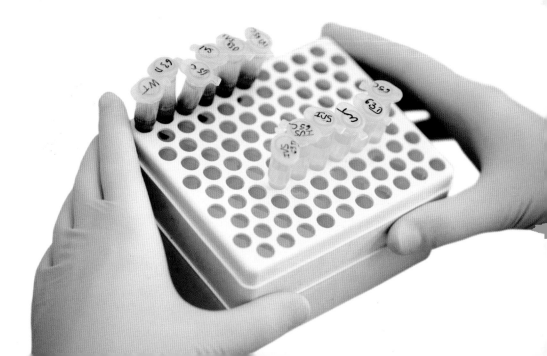

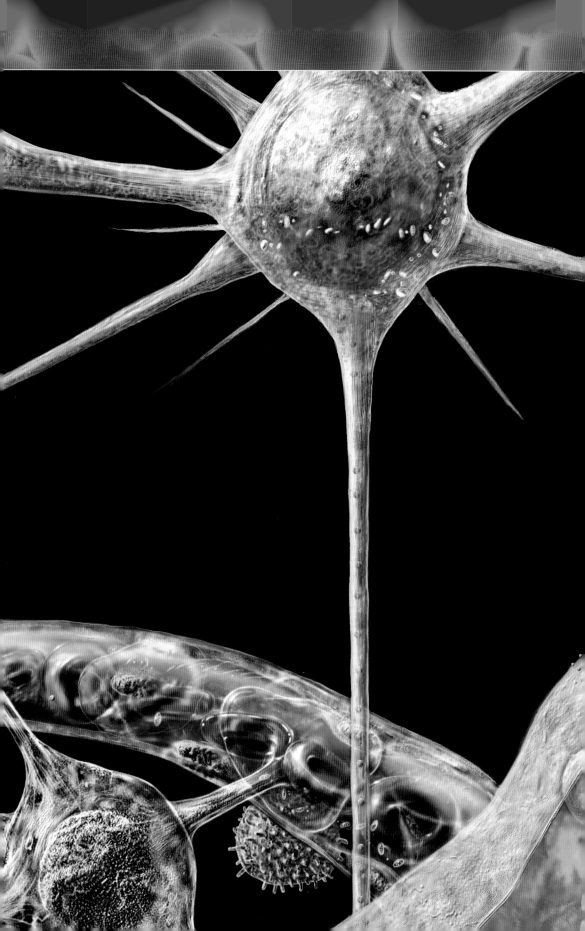

Medical Mysteries

Science Researches Conditions from Bizarre to Deadly

By Scott Auden

Dr. Elizabeth Brownell, Consultant

NATIONAL
GEOGRAPHIC

Washington, D.C.

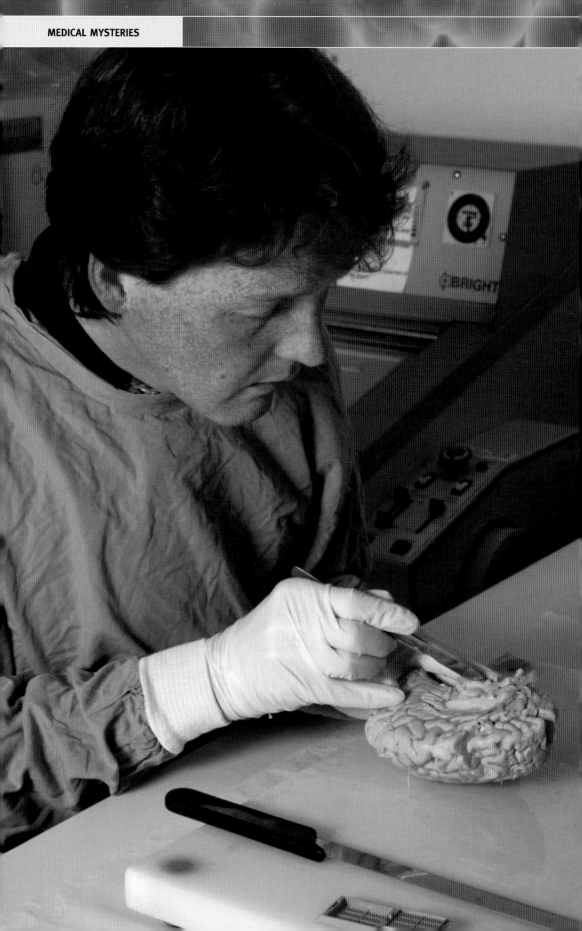

Contents

Message from the Consultant   **8**

Timeline of Major Medical Mysteries   **10**

 Medical Science   **12**

Pathology • Genetics • Heredity • Classification • Physiology • Hippocrates

 Pathology   **20**

A new threat • The laughing death • What went wrong? • Mad cow disease • vCJD cases on the rise

 Genetics   **28**

Putting up a fight • DNA • Trying for a cure

 Heredity   **34**

Bizarre symptoms • Hundreds of years of mystery • Eastlack's legacy • Commitment to a cure • Complications • IFOPA • Discovery at last

< A researcher dissects a human brain, studying its shape, size, and structure in order to diagnose brain disorders including Alzheimer's disease, Parkinson's disease, and Creutzfeldt-Jakob disease.

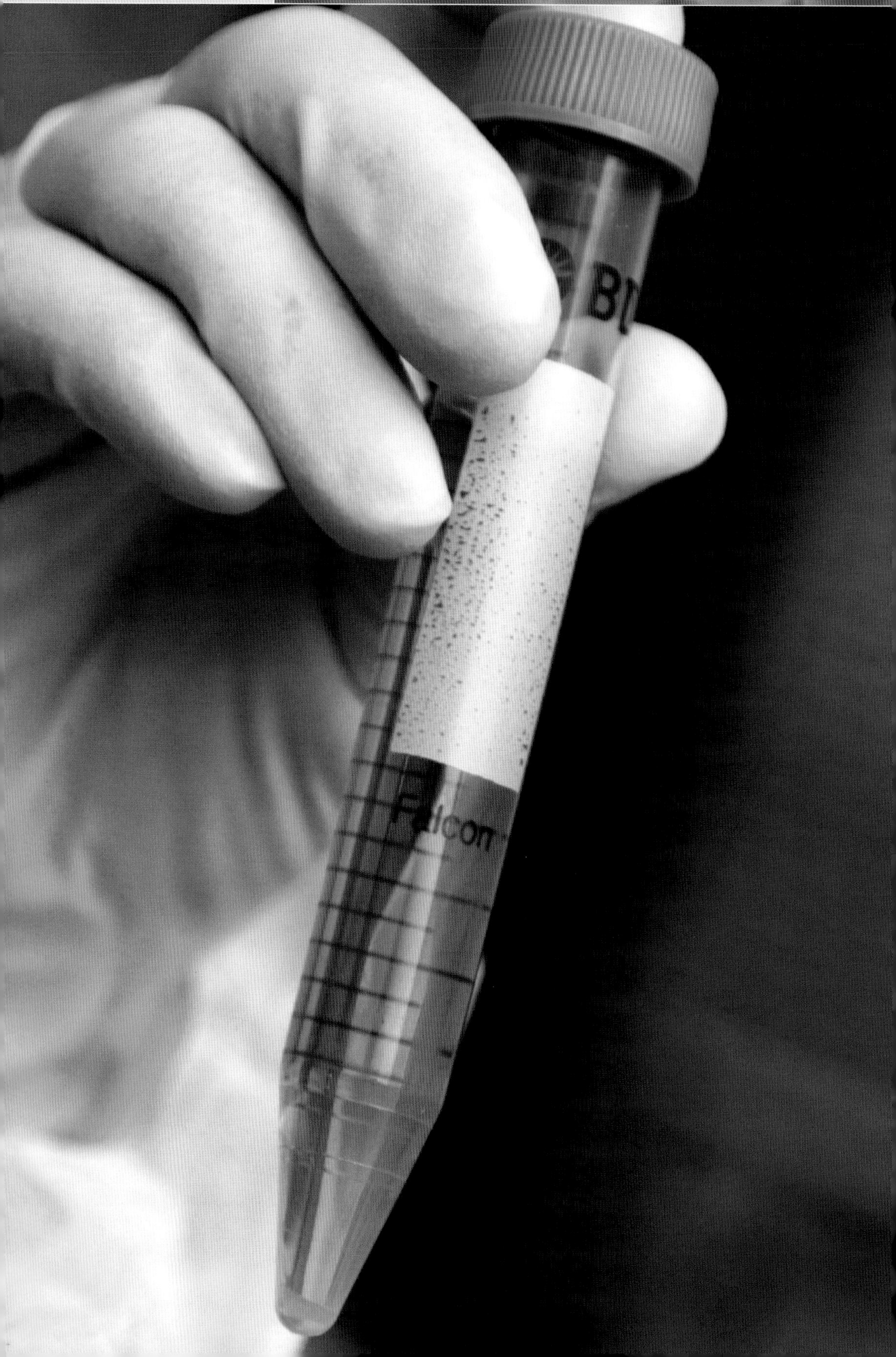
BD
Falcon

5 Classification 42

A mystery • Searching for help • A growing body of
evidence • Skepticism and the scientific method
• Meet a medical researcher

6 Physiology 50

Learning from surgery • Early research • Are you a
righty? • First, do no harm • Left- or right-brained

The Years Ahead	58
Glossary	59
Bibliography	60
On the Web	60
Index	61
About the Author and Consultant	63
Credits	64

< The genetic material in this test tube can be analyzed and decoded thanks to the Human Genome
Project, which created a map identifying the more than 20,000 genes in the human body.

From the Consultant

Being a doctor is like being a detective trying to find all the right clues to solve a mystery, a medical mystery!

I am a family doctor, which means that I take care of all ages and types of patients from babies to grandparents. There are medical mysteries to be solved everyday at the clinic—some easy and some not so easy. But a doctor can't do it alone. It takes the help of many different scientists, medical researchers, and medical specialists to piece together the clues to solve the puzzle. It takes a lot of teamwork and the goal is always to help the patient.

On my first day of medical school my anatomy professor told us that we would "be in school forever"—and he was right! The study of medicine and disease changes constantly and there is always something new to be learned and researched. Medicine is always challenging, but never dull.

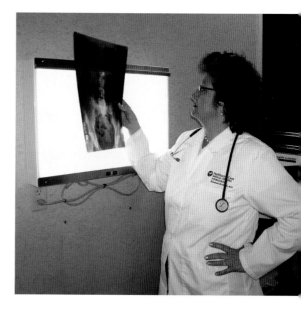

If you like a challenge like I do, you'll be amazed and inspired by the medical mysteries discussed in this book and the dedication of all those involved in solving them.

Elizabeth E. Brownell, MD
Wisconsin, 2008

> The human body is amazing, and complicated. Understanding how eleven different body systems, such as the circulatory system (left) and the nervous system (right) normally work is important when someone gets sick.

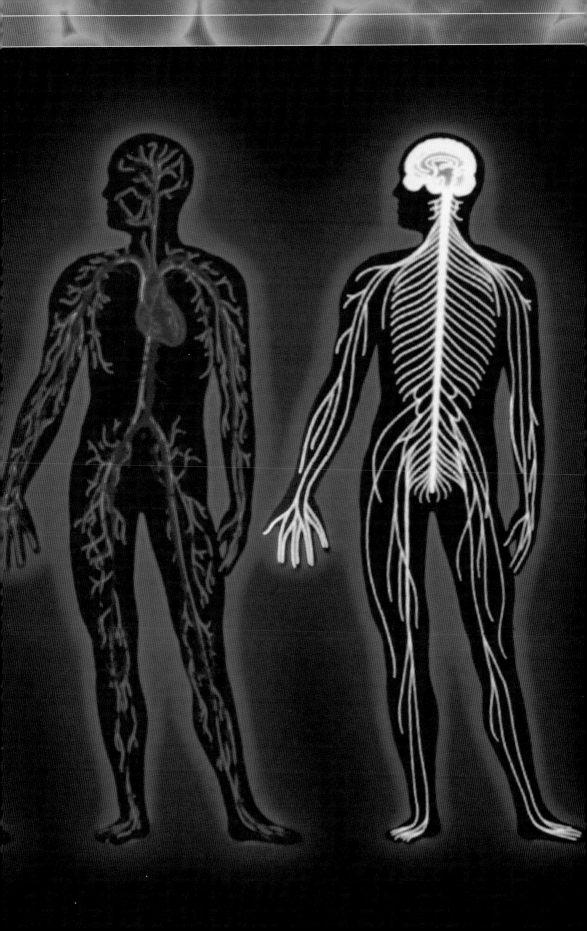

< **1860** · Gustav Fechner is the first scientist to theorize that the brain had control of two different parts of one's body.

> **1980s** · Cows in the United Kingdom are herded into sheds to be tested for bovine spongiform encephalopathy, also known as mad cow disease.

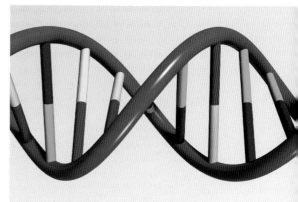

> **1953** · An illustration shows the unique double helix structure of DNA discovered by Drs. Watson and Crick.

1690   1740   1860   1950

1692

Fibrodysplasia ossificans progressiva (FOP) is first mentioned in the scientific literature by French doctor Guy Patin

1740

Dr. John Freke describes a 14-year-old FOP patient in a scientific paper

1860

Gustav Fechner theorizes that each hemisphere of the brain has its own consciousness

1953

Biologists unlock the mystery of the structure of deoxyribonucleic acid (DNA), the molecule that constitutes the building block of life

1950s

Kuru, also known as the laughing death, is studied among the Fore people of Papua New Guinea

> **2003** · The seal of the Human Genome Project, the international effort by researchers and scientists to identify all the genes in the human body. The success of the project will lead to new treatments and approaches in biology, medicine, and agriculture.

V **2006** · Scientists begin to investigate Morgellons disease, an affliction that has been the source of controversy in the medical community. Verna Gallagher believes she has the disease.

1980	2000

1981

Roger Sperry receives the Nobel Prize for his work with split-brain patients

1982

Stanley Prusiner identifies the prion, a previously unknown agent of disease

2006

Scientists at the Centers for Disease Control and Prevention begin investigation of Morgellons disease

2006

Frederick Kaplan and Eileen Shore identify the gene involved in FOP.

1980s

An epidemic of mad cow disease strikes livestock in the United Kingdom

2003

Francis Collins discovers the genetic cause of progeria, a rare disease in which the aging process is greatly accelerated

The Human Genome Project finishes mapping the human genome

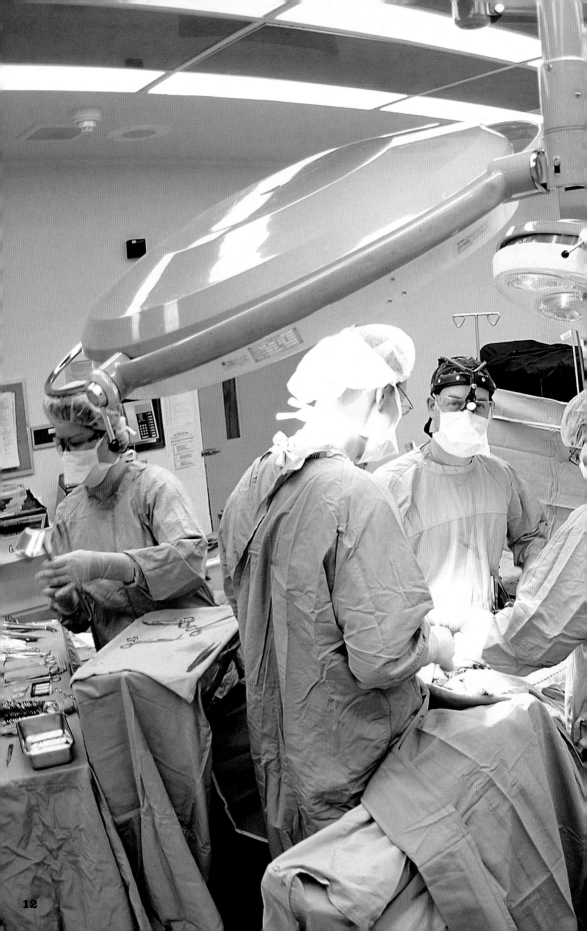

CHAPTER 1

Medical Science

Studying Disease

S cience is a tool for understanding the world around us. It is a special way of asking and answering questions designed to help us figure out how things work. Medical science, in turn, is a way for human beings to understand themselves. It is true that every man, woman, and child is unique. But the ways our bodies work, grow, and sometimes malfunction are the same no matter where we are from or what we look like.

The human body is many, many times more complicated than any machine or system ever designed by people. After hundreds of years of effort by thousands and thousands of individuals, we have only just begun to understand how the body works.

< Doctors from various disciplines are involved in surgery on a patient. It often takes the help of experts in several fields working together to treat and cure illness.

It is pretty complicated. If medicine, like other sciences, were driven mostly by curiosity or profit, it might be hard to understand why scientists put so much effort into it. But medical science is vitally important in a way that many other kinds of research are not. When people get sick, they suffer. Sometimes, they die. At its core, medical research is about preventing suffering and death. By using science to understand what is happening when people have a disease, researchers can often figure out how to prevent and cure sickness.

Because the human body is so complex, there are many, many

∧ Abnormal cells are grown in petri dishes and later examined by pathologists looking to unlock the secrets of a particular disease.

∨ A pathologist examines samples on a slide under a microscope. Pathology is the study of disease. A pathologist spends most of the time in the laboratory and provides valuable information to doctors treating patients with all sorts of diseases.

∧ A jar containing tissue samples will be analyzed by pathologists for the presence of pathogens that might cause disease.

different disciplines, or types, of medical science. Each specialty focuses on one specific part of the fight against sickness, but as our understanding of the human body progresses, the different parts of study overlap. This book takes a look at diseases that fall into five different disciplines.

Pathology

Pathology is the study of disease. Scientists who specialize in this branch of medical research are called pathologists. Pathologists try to understand what is happening when something goes wrong in the human body. Diseases have many different causes and can affect the body in countless ways. Pathologists figure out and keep track of as many of these causes and effects as they can. Preventing a disease can be all but impossible without knowing what is causing the disease and how it is being transmitted from one person to another. Until early pathologists had learned what caused infection, surgeons did not even bother to wash their hands or to sterilize their equipment before operating. In Chapter 2, you will read about how the work of pathologists led to the discovery of one of the ways diseases are spread: the prion. Pathology could not exist, however, by itself. Without an understanding of other fields of medicine, pathologists would have no place to start.

Genetics

Our bodies, complicated as they are, come with a complete set of instructions for development. These directions are contained within nearly every single cell of the body. The tiniest drop of blood has millions of copies of the complete instructions, providing "blueprints" for processes throughout the system. Scientists cannot read all the instructions yet, but they learn more every day. The information is contained in structures called chromosomes, and each individual bit of instruction in a chromosome is called a gene. The discipline that studies genes is called genetics. Genetics is important to medicine, because sometimes disease is caused by a mistake in a copy of these genetic instructions.

Read Chapter 3 to learn about genetic research and the exploration of a treatment to combat a genetic disease called progeria.

Λ A scientist in his lab tests cancer cells in an effort to develop a vaccine against the widespread disease. It is hoped that the vaccine will use the body's own genetic material to fight the abnormal cancer cells.

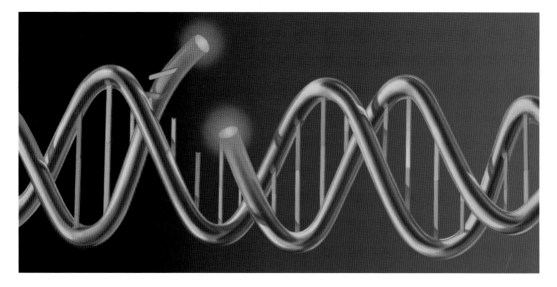

Λ Our cells contain DNA, which carries thousands of genes that provide instructions for how our body functions. Disease often results from a defect in a particular gene, as shown here.

Heredity

Closely related to genetics is the study of heredity. You inherit your genes from your parents—half of your chromosomes from your mother and half from your father. That is why you show the traits of both your parents. Some diseases are labeled hereditary because the genes that cause the disease can be passed from parent to child. You do not catch the disease as you would catch a cold; you are born with it, or with the potential for it, because that particular disease is a trait passed on to you by your parents, just like the color of your skin and the shape of your nose. Chapter 4 looks at a hereditary genetic disease called fibrodysplasia ossificans progressiva (FOP) and the work being done to understand and cure it.

Classification

There are many different kinds of illness and disease. There are so many that just classifying what is and is not a disease, and what types of diseases there are, is a discipline all its own. These classifications are more than just organization. There are only so many ways the body breaks down, but there are countless reasons that cause it to break down. Everyone has had a headache or a stomachache. There are literally hundreds of things that can cause a headache or stomachache—some serious, some

∧ Members of the Norman family have a disease that has been classified as genetic. It has been passed on to seven family members and more may be at risk.

not. Classification helps to clarify when you should be worried and when you need only to take two aspirin and lie down. Also, new diseases appear from time to time. If a new disease has symptoms similar to a well-known one, doctors might misunderstand the causes of the symptoms and give the wrong treatment. Read Chapter 5 to find out about the fascinating debate surrounding what some scientists (and patients) think is a new disease called Morgellons.

Physiology

The discipline that deals with understanding how the body is put together, and how it works, is called physiology. Some of the basic systems in the human body, like the skeleton and the veins and arteries of the circulatory system, are well understood. Other parts, like the brain and nervous system, are still very mysterious. As science and technology provide tools to look at the body in more and more detail, scientists continue to discover more and more levels of complexity beneath what they thought they already understood. New systems, too small to be seen before, are revealed every time someone invents a better kind of microscope. And the ways those

< An exhibition titled "Bodies...The Exhibition" shows various preserved human specimens, some with normal bodily processes and others with varying diseases.

Hippocrates

No one man or woman is responsible for the shape of modern medicine. But if you had to pick one, Hippocrates would be a pretty good choice. He was a Greek doctor on an island called Kos in the third century B.C. He was one of the first to insist that diseases were natural phenomena that could be understood and prevented, rather than supernatural punishments from angry gods and spirits. He included the very modern idea that environmental factors were a consideration in understanding disease, considering such influences as water quality and local weather conditions. He collected detailed case histories of various diseases to help his research. He thought if he observed enough cases, he could learn to predict the course of the disease. He was right, of course. Among Hippocrates' other radical ideas was the notion that staying clean could contribute to keeping you healthy. Simply put, he had so many good ideas about medicine that after more than 2,000 years his thinking on the topic is still the accepted wisdom. To this day, most doctors still swear an oath to be good doctors, called the Hippocratic Oath.

∧ Hippocrates is sometimes called the "father of medicine," because his theories of disease and medical protocol are still practiced today.

systems interact with each other are revealed every time scientists study the results of an accident, a disease, or a surgical procedure. Chapter 6 reviews work that physiologists are doing to understand the brain's structure and how it affects the way we think and see the world.

In a way, all medical research is personal. Scientists, after all, are human. They get sick, and their loved ones get sick, just as we do. When we become ill, we go to the doctor. But it is the medical researchers who, in a sense, tell the doctors what to do, so they can help us.

Pathology

CHAPTER 2

The Laughing Death

Imagine spending your day going to school or work, relaxing in the park, shopping for groceries, and eating dinner, all the while not knowing that you are living with an incurable, fatal disease. Researchers such as Dr. John Collinge at University College London think that hundreds of thousands of people might be doing exactly that! It is possible that an invisible epidemic has taken root in the United Kingdom. A disease called variant Creutzfeldt-Jakob disease (vCJD) may have infected people who do not even know they have it...yet.

Thanks to the work of hundreds of pathologists over the years, doctors today understand quite a bit about how most diseases are transmitted.

< Tissue samples taken from the brains of cows with bovine spongiform encephalopathy (mad cow disease) are stored for analysis and study.

Bacteria, viruses, and various parasites are well known, and strategies for fighting them are well established. But vCJD is transmitted by something far newer to science: the prion.

A New Threat

The name "prion" means a proteinaceous infectious particle. It was first identified in 1982 by the American neurologist Stanley B. Prusiner. Prusiner and other scientists had been trying to find the cause of scrapie, a degenerative

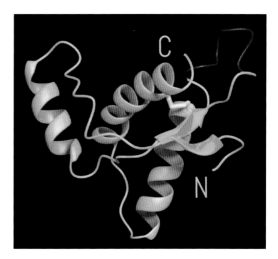

∧ A three-dimensional model of a prion. The letter N marks the beginning of the abnormal protein and C indicates the end of it.

∨ A veterinarian takes a sample of a sheep's saliva to test for evidence of scrapie, a known prion disease that strikes animals. Researchers studying scrapie discovered evidence of prions when efforts to kill off all living matter in the sample failed to stop the disease.

disease of the nervous system that kills sheep.

They knew scrapie had something to do with brain tissue. Brain tissue taken from a sick sheep and injected into a healthy one would cause scrapie. Experimenters tried to isolate exactly what substance in the tissue was causing the infection by treating the tissue in different ways intended to remove a likely culprit. If they killed the bacteria in the tissue, for example, and if it still infected a healthy sheep, they knew scrapie was not caused by bacteria. Finally, an experimenter named Tikvah Alper tried bombarding the tissue with enough radiation to destroy anything alive. The researchers were astonished to find that the tissue was still infectious, even though there was no way any bacterium or virus could have survived.

Prusiner then discovered that when he treated the brain tissue samples in such a way that proteins in them would be destroyed, the samples would no longer cause scrapie. He concluded that a protein was carrying the disease. Dr. Prusiner received the Nobel Prize for medicine in 1997.

It turns out that abnormal prions are very similar to a kind of protein molecule that is normally found in the brain and nervous system. They attach themselves to healthy brain cell proteins and alter their shape. As these proteins change shape, they cause damage to brain tissue, leaving it riddled with holes, like a sponge. Mental abilities break down, as does the ability to control the body. Common symptoms include changes in personality, confusion, delirium, memory loss, uncontrollable body tremors, and paralysis. Death always follows.

∧ **Dr. Stanley B. Prusiner (left) is presented with the Nobel Prize for medicine in 1997 by Swedish King Carl XVI Gustaf in Stockholm, Sweden.**

The Laughing Death

The first human prion disease to be studied was found in the 1950s in an isolated community in the jungles of Papua New Guinea, a country of offshore islands located in the southwestern Pacific Ocean. The people of the Fore tribe were suffering terribly from a disease called kuru, which in the Fore language means "trembling with fear." It began with headaches and joint pain and then progressed to body tremors, confusion, memory loss, and uncontrollable laughter. For this reason it was sometimes called the laughing death. Within no more than two years, victims would die paralyzed, with masklike smiles frozen on their faces. Kuru killed more than 50 percent of the women and children of the tribe.

In the 1950s prions were still unknown to scientists. An American anthropologist named Daniel Carleton Gajdusek, who also happened to be a medical doctor, finally figured out how kuru was transmitted while he was living among the Fore. The Fore people had a cultural practice of funeral cannibalism. As a sign of respect, the mourners ate parts of the dead, including the brain. Prions, it turns out, can enter the body by being eaten. When the Australian government (which had authority in New Guinea) outlawed cannibalism in the 1960s, kuru began to disappear, confirming Dr. Gajdusek's theory. Today, kuru is extremely rare.

Mad Cow Disease

Despite the suffering of the Fore, prion diseases have been extremely rare in human beings. They are more common among animals. Perhaps the most well-known

What Went Wrong?

Most of the things that can cause a contagious disease by invading your body are alive or at least share qualities with living things. Parasites of various species are essentially animals that are using your body as their habitat and food source. Bacteria are single-celled organisms that can be seen only with a microscope. You might also be infected by other single-cell creatures like protozoa or by fungi, which are more like plants.

Viruses, which are many times smaller than the smallest bacteria, are not actually alive, but they do have a lot in common with living things. By infecting a healthy cell and using it to create copies of themselves, viruses reproduce and evolve.

A prion is not a living thing; it consists of protein only and lacks the genetic material contained in living things. A prion molecule can exist for years outside the body and still be infectious if it invades a living thing. Prions are also resistant to most techniques used to sterilize hospital equipment. At the moment, there is no known cure for any prion disease.

∧ The front pages of newspapers in London in 1996 illustrate the fear felt by the public when it was announced that a strain of Creuztfeldt-Jakob disease was linked to mad cow disease.

prion disease is bovine spongiform encephalopathy (BSE), also known as mad cow disease. BSE is so well known largely because of a massive outbreak in the United Kingdom in the 1980s. The outbreak was fueled the same way kuru had been among the Fore. It was common for cows to be fed protein supplements made from leftover parts of slaughtered cows, as well as sheep. Unknown to anyone, some of the slaughtered livestock had been infected with BSE. The protein taken from these carcasses and fed to healthy livestock included prions. Healthy cows soon became sick from ingesting prions within the supplements.

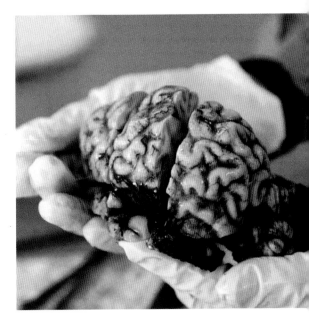

∧ The brain of a cow is inspected for signs of bovine spongiform encephalopathy, also known as mad cow disease.

∧ An employee at a meat processing plant in Germany in November 2000 inspects beef carcasses in cold storage for signs of disease. The tissue is waiting to be tested for BSE (mad cow disease), which has rocked the beef industry in Europe since 1996.

vCJD Cases on the Rise

Recently, there have been very disturbing signs that the BSE outbreak of the 1980s might have had a much greater impact on people than was realized. For 40 years, scientists have known about Creutzfeldt-Jakob disease (CJD), a rare prion disease affecting humans. Recently, a new or variant form of CJD, called vCJD, has emerged in Great Britain. Sometimes,

a "new" disease only seems new because it has just recently begun to affect humans. It may have been infecting certain species of animals for a very long time, but never before "jumped" to people. A disease that spreads from animals to people is called a zoonosis. Evidence is beginning to suggest that vCJD is a zoonosis afflicting humans who ate beef infected with BSE.

Since 1996, when vCJD was first reported, almost 200 cases have been recorded. All the cases were fatal, and scientists believe that all the patients with the disease were infected by eating diseased beef. vCJD is not contagious and cannot be passed from human to human. Laws have been passed to prevent possible new infections, including outlawing the practice of feeding slaughtered animal parts to live cows intended for the marketplace.

What is most disturbing about the situation is that no one is certain how many people have been infected. Prion diseases have extremely long incubation times. That means it can be many years between the time you're infected and when you first show symptoms. John Collinge's work at University College London deals with this. Realizing that the only known major outbreak of a human prion disease could tell them much about what to expect with vCJD, he and his colleagues took another long look at the Fore people. Although the practice of cannibalism has been gone for 40 years, kuru took much longer to die out. Collinge has concluded that an average incubation time is probably about 12 years, but an incubation of as much as 50 years is not unlikely depending on the victim. That means that we will find out over the next 20 years how much damage was done by the BSE outbreak in the 1980s. Estimates run from hundreds of people infected all the way up to millions.

> The British public awaits the outcome of the mad cow disease scare, which may not be known for 20 years.

∧ Rajiv Singh, a physics professor at the University of California—Davis, holds up a slide illustrating a human protein cell. Singh is studying mad cow disease and Creutzfeldt-Jakob disease using computer modeling. The computer screen shows a model of infected cells.

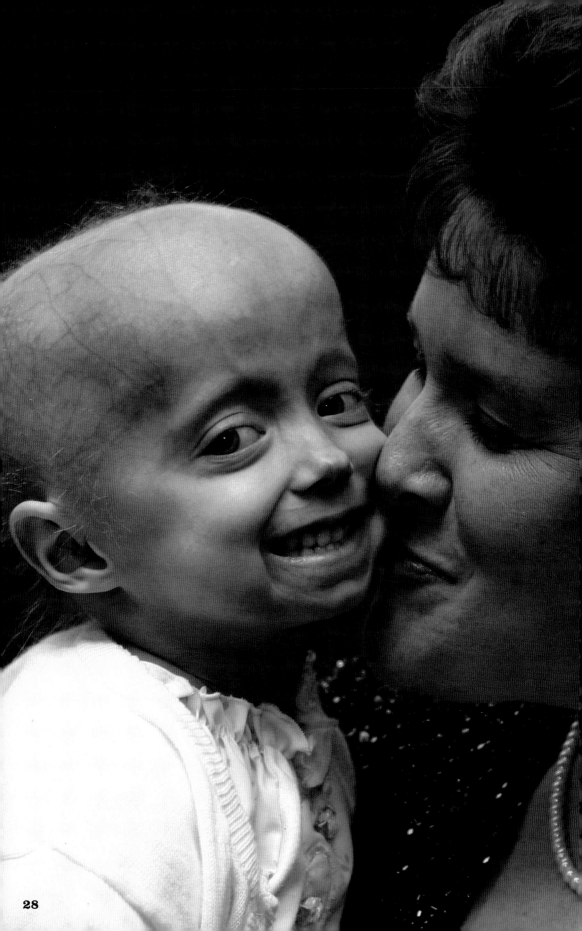

Genetics

CHAPTER 3

Little Old Boys and Girls

When Sam Berns was born, he seemed to be a fine, healthy baby. Sam's body began to grow and develop, following the genetic blueprint, or set of directions, his cells mapped out. All humans have such a blueprint, and, usually, it leads to a healthy, normal body. When Sam was 21 months old, however, he was diagnosed with a rare, fatal disorder called progeria.

Progeria affects only about one child in eight million; roughly 40 children in the world are known to have the disease at a given time. Progeria is not passed down in families because the condition is caused by a new and random gene mutation. When Sam was diagnosed, very little was known

< Megan, a child with progeria, poses with her mother. Progeria is the result of an error in a cell's DNA that causes the body to age rapidly.

about progeria. There were no medical or research foundations conducting drug trials, no major research efforts to speak of. The disease was so rare that it did not seem to merit much attention, or research money, from the scientific community. Sam's parents, however, were both doctors. And if the rest of the medical community was not interested in progeria, they certainly were.

The word "progeria" comes from the Greek word *geras,* meaning "old age." Progeria's symptoms are unmistakable. The disorder causes a child to appear very old, even at ages as young as five years. Though the child appears normal as a newborn, within a year growth slows dramatically. Then, the children lose most of their fat, their hair falls out, and their skin becomes thin and stiff. These young children may suffer from stiffness of the joints or hip dislocations. The children die of heart disease between the ages of seven and nineteen. Though progeria causes rapid aging of the body, it does not interfere with intellectual development.

▼ John Tacket, 16 years old, PRF Youth Ambassador, of Bay City, Michigan speaks to the media about growing up with progeria during a news conference in April 2003 to announce the discovery of the gene that causes this rare disease. His parents stand behind him.

Putting Up a Fight

Sam's parents, Dr. Leslie Gordon and Dr. Sam Berns, started the Progeria Research Foundation (PRF), an organization devoted to finding the cause, treatment, and cure for progeria. Sam's mother, Dr. Gordon, devoted herself to battling progeria full-time. Once the foundation was established, Dr. Gordon began collecting samples of cells from children with progeria so that researchers would have the biological tools they would need to conduct their research. She contacted families around the world who had a child with progeria and asked them to supply tissue samples. The result of this early effort was the creation of the PRF tissue bank. Dr. Gordon then formed a scientific group whose goal was to find the genetic mutation for progeria. A genetic mutation is a variation in the normal makeup of a gene. She enlisted the help of Dr. Francis Collins, a geneticist at the National Institutes of Health.

∧ Dr. Leslie Gordon, in her lab, conducts research on progeria, the genetic disease her son, Sam, was born with.

Dr. Collins compared the tissue samples from children with progeria to healthy genetic samples. Within a year, the scientific group found a common element among the children with progeria. There was a tiny error in their DNA. Nearly all the progeria tissue samples had the same error in the instructions the body uses to grow and mature properly.

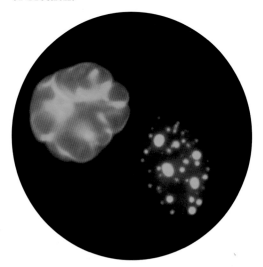

< Untreated cells from children with the genetic disease progeria (left) compared to similar cells treated with farnesyltransferase inhibitors (FTIs). In the test tube, FTIs reverse the cell damage caused by the disease.

DNA

DNA, which stands for deoxyribonucleic acid, is like a blueprint for a living thing. These blueprints contain instructions for how the body must put itself together. Imagine a construction blueprint for a building that specified not only the materials and measurements to use, but the instructions for how each screw should be turned, how each nail should be driven, and how each plumbing and light fixture should be made before it was installed. Then remember that the human body is vastly more complex than any building, and you will have an idea how much information is contained within DNA.

A gene is a section of DNA that encodes some particular trait you could inherit from your mother or father. The chemicals in a DNA molecule are packed into structures called chromosomes, which are in the center of most of the cells in your body. Chromosomes occur in pairs, each pair made up of one copy of each parent's DNA. Humans have 23 pairs of chromosomes; taken together, the resulting blueprint is a combination of both parents' traits. By learning where on each chromosome a particular gene is found, scientists are beginning to be able to read the genetic blueprint and identify which genes are involved with which traits. They are also learning which pairs are involved in certain diseases.

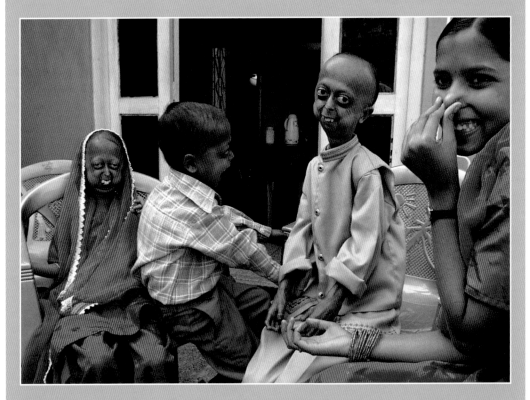

∧ Three out of four children in the Khan family of Calcutta, India, suffer from progeria, the genetic disease that speeds the body's aging process. The Khan family is unique in that they are the only known family where more than one member has the disease.

A particular gene was supposed to make a protein that created a framework for the wall of the nucleus (a cell's nucleus contains most of its genetic material and helps the cell to function normally). In progeria patients, however, some of the protein was abnormal, and the wall of the nucleus was not as strong as it should have been. Cells that undergo a lot of stress, such as in the blood vessels, might therefore fail. This finding could explain the heart disease seen in progeria patients. As a result of this discovery, PRF created a genetic testing program for progeria and now tests children all over the globe.

Trying for a Cure

The most exciting news about the discovery of the genetic root of progeria was that it was now possible to start examining ideas for potential treatments or cures. If researchers could correct the faulty protein somehow, they might be able to address the disease as well. A drug called farnesyltransferase inhibitor (FTI), which had originally been developed to treat cancer, seemed likely to operate against the defective protein in progeria as well. This was a brilliant stroke of luck. The drug had already been through the very lengthy process of government approval. (All medicines in the United States must go through a testing and approval process by the government

that sometimes takes decades.) Any drug created from scratch to treat progeria would have taken years to be tested before it got anywhere near a real progeria patient. As it is, there were several nonhuman tests performed first, all of which seemed very encouraging. Mice that had been given the progeria mutation and developed symptoms similar to progeria responded very well to the FTI, surviving longer or not exhibiting some of the debilitating symptoms.

In May 2007, Dr. Gordon helped launch the first clinical trials of FTI for the treatment of progeria. Since the discovery of the gene responsible for progeria, there has been no shortage of research focusing on the disease. A new understanding of abnormal aging and heart disease may open up our understanding of normal aging. Researchers are examining the genes of people who have lived into their 90s and beyond to see if there is a relationship between the progeria gene and longevity. Studying one of the rarest diseases on Earth may have already provided clues about how all humans age.

These days Sam Bern acts like any other kid. He likes to run and play, read books, make Lego models, and play baseball. His eyesight, however, is starting to fail and his joints are beginning to stiffen. His body age is now about ten times his actual age.

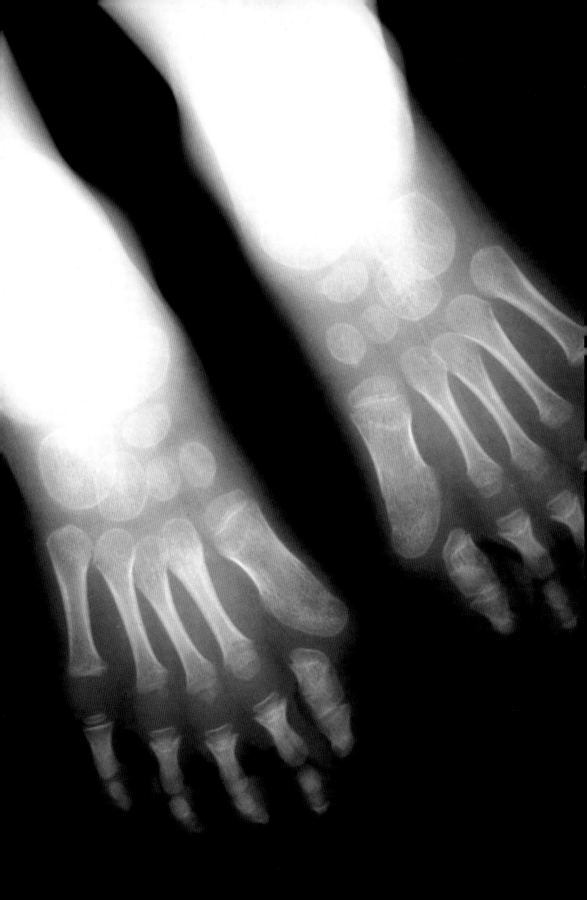

Heredity

CHAPTER 4

Dangerous Transformation

When Harry Eastlack was born, his parents noticed that there was something wrong with his big toe. It was slightly deformed. Otherwise, Harry seemed like a healthy and normal baby. And, in most ways he always would be. But gradually, tragically, Harry's family realized that he was one of the very unlucky few suffering from an extremely rare hereditary genetic disorder called fibrodysplasia ossificans progressiva (FOP). From the age of 10, Harry Eastlack's body began to ossify, or turn to stone. By the time he was 39, Harry was able to move only his lips.

◁ An x-ray of the foot of a child born with FOP shows a malformation of the big toe. This deformity is the first sign of the disease.

Bizarre Symptoms

First came painful swellings on Harry's body, beginning when he was still a young child. They were warm to the touch. Sometimes they appeared without any obvious cause. Other times they formed where Harry had injuries, and each bump and scrape, normal enough for any child, became a matter of concern. When a doctor was finally consulted, Harry's parents were astounded. Harry's bumps were new bones forming where new bones should never form.

As Harry grew, his intelligence was unaffected. He was even expected to live a long life. But the gradual loss of mobility as his body tried to grow a second skeleton led to some real challenges. Limited mobility would make actions as ordinary as riding a bicycle impossible. He might be frozen into a standing position and never again be able to sit down. A fused jaw could make eating impossible. A loss of mobility in his chest could mean that his heart or lungs would not be free to move as they needed to. Harry's condition would continue to worsen.

Hundreds of Years of Mystery

FOP was first identified in the 17th century. The French physician Guy Patin wrote in 1692 about a patient who "finally became as hard as wood

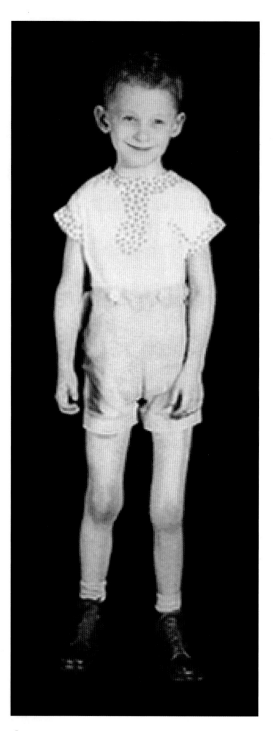

∧ Harry Eastlack as a boy, before the effects of FOP completely took over his body and affected his mobility. By the time he was a grown man, the only part of the body Eastlack could move was his lips.

Eastlack's Legacy

When Harry Eastlack died of pneumonia in 1973, just a few days shy of his 40th birthday, he changed the course of study and research for one of science's most puzzling mysteries. Although many scientists who study FOP are intimately familiar with Eastlack's case, few ever had the chance to meet him personally. In the final days of his life, Harry Eastlack made a profoundly generous gesture. Hoping that people in the future would not have to suffer as he had throughout his life, he arranged that, when he died, his skeleton, severely deformed by FOP, should be donated to the doctors who had treated him. Today, Eastlack's skeleton is displayed in the Mutter Museum of the College of Physicians in Philadelphia.

A normal skeleton must be assembled and held together with wire before it can be displayed. Eastlack's story can be read in the shape of his skeleton, which is so heavily fused together that little such assembly was needed to mount and display it. Many scientists who are working to treat FOP all over the world come to consult this important research tool.

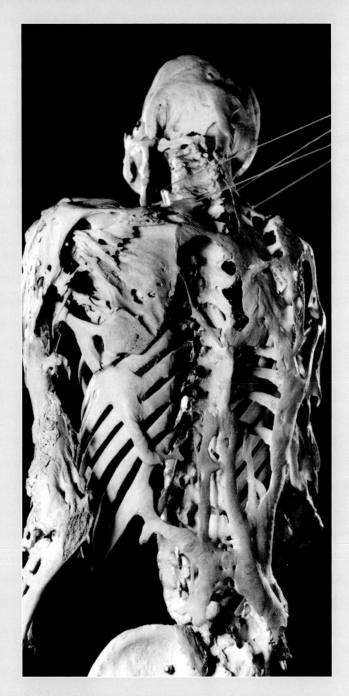

∧ The skeleton of Harry Eastlack is on display at the Mutter Museum of the College of Physicians in Philadelphia. Scientists around the world use Eastlack's skeleton as a tool for studying and understanding FOP.

all over." Many doctors since then have also compared the creeping immobility of FOP to a person's slowly turning into stone or wood.

FOP affects about one in every two million people. As sometimes happens with very rare diseases, research was slow to develop. There is no mention of FOP in scientific writings between Guy Patin's first reference in 1692 and 1740, when a doctor named John Freke described a 14-year-old patient. The boy had large swellings all down his back, many the size of a small loaf of bread. They arose from every rib in his body and joined at the back.

Commitment to a Cure

In 1977, Dr. Michael Zasloff walked into his exam room to see an eight-year-old child. She had been enjoying herself at an amusement park, like many other children. But when her neck whipped around on one of the rides, she developed swelling in the region that was clearly causing her great pain. Zasloff knew that this girl had FOP. His boss, Dr. Victor McKusick, had written one of the definitive textbooks on the mysterious disease. But FOP

was still largely a puzzle that many doctors overlooked. Moved by the suffering of this young girl, Dr. Zasloff committed himself to understanding the disorder.

Although it is hereditary, FOP often appears in a newborn whose parents show no sign of the disease. There are usually no symptoms at first, except a characteristic deformity of the big toes. It is likely that whatever gene is causing the abnormal bone growth is also in control of the shape of the big toe.

As children with FOP get older, they begin to experience swelling in various places on their body. As the swelling goes down, a bone is usually found to have grown in its place. The bones are completely normal in their makeup. But the bone growth in FOP usually begins in muscles or ligaments, parts of the body that need to be flexible in order to function. When these muscles and ligaments harden into bone, they usually lose their mobility, and the patient's body loses a little of its ability to move.

In the late 1980s, Zasloff attended a talk by

> Children with FOP appear normal at birth with the exception of their big toes. Now that scientists understand that this is a sign of the disease, they can begin evaluating their patients at a much earlier age than before.

 Dr. Frederick Kaplan with a 15-year-old FOP patient in his lab at the University of Pennsylvania School of Medicine. Dr. Kaplan, along with his colleague Dr. Eileen Shore, found what they called the "skeleton key" to FOP when they discovered the gene responsible for FOP in 2006.

Frederick Kaplan, a doctor at the University of Pennsylvania in Philadelphia. Kaplan had two FOP patients and no clear idea about how FOP behaved. The two men decided to work together. As they began to organize their data, they noticed a pattern that everyone else had missed. Flare-ups of bone tended to develop in patients in the same order—first in the neck and spine, then the shoulders, then hips and elbows, followed finally by the knees, wrists, and ankles. The last thing likely to be affected was the jaw. Zasloff and Kaplan recognized the pattern at once. The flare-ups were following the same pattern of bone growth seen in developing newborns. It seemed likely that FOP bone growth could be related to the process that maps out the pattern of how a normal baby's bones grow. It is interesting that the muscles of the heart, tongue, eyes, and diaphragm are not affected by FOP.

Complications

Complicating the search for a treatment for FOP is the fact that FOP seems to react to any kind of trauma or injury to the body.

This is the reason why extra bone cannot be removed by surgery. The surgery, which is after all a controlled "injury" to the body, typically leads to even worse bone growth than before. This has led some scientists to conclude that FOP bone growth is also related to the way a body repairs itself. It would be as if the body's healing process has malfunctioned and instead of repairing the tissue as it should, it replaces it with bone. To stop the disease, one can't remove the bone. One has to keep it from growing in the first place.

In the late 1990s, Zasloff concentrated on ways to halt bone growth. His research focused on an unlikely subject: sharks. Sharks' bodies are made up of cartilage rather than bones. Zasloff found that a unique mechanism controls the growth of cartilage and prevents it from hardening into bones by restricting blood flow to the shark's tissues. A drug derived from sharks could work in humans with FOP to keep their flare-ups from actually

IFOPA

The International Fibrodysplasia Ossificans Progressiva Association (IFOPA) has a website where you can learn more about this strange disease that imprisons people within their own bodies. Because of its rarity, FOP is commonly misdiagnosed. Many patients are thought to have cancer because the lesions or growths associated with FOP are often believed to be tumors. The FOP website gives in-depth, easy-to-understand explanations of the symptoms and directions for what to do if you think someone you know has FOP. It also offers news and updates on the latest research and best hope for people with this disease. If you have a friend with FOP, the IFOPA website also has a section describing what it is like for kids with FOP, how it affects them in school, and what things will change and stay the same about your friend as the disease gets worse.

becoming bone. This type of treatment would attack the consequences of the disease; however, it was clear that the best, most effective treatment would target the root cause of FOP.

∧ Dr. Eileen Shore and research specialist Meiqi Xu, in the FOP research laboratory at the University of Pennsylvania, contributed to the discovery of the FOP gene mutation.

Discovery at Last

Since 1991, when Dr. Eileen Shore joined the FOP team, Dr. Kaplan and Dr. Shore have focused on the root of the problem. They realized that FOP was almost certainly a genetic disorder. In 2006, after many years of work at the University of Pennsylvania School of Medicine, Kaplan and Shore announced that they had found the key, or, as they called it, the "skeleton key," to the mystery of FOP. They had managed to identify the precise gene that causes FOP. With that information, Kaplan and Shore were also able to identify the protein that manages bone growth in the body. Changes in that protein are what cause FOP sufferers' bone growth to go out of control.

Unfortunately, there is still no known way to prevent FOP. An understanding of the genetics behind bone growth, normal or abnormal, holds the answer. And it is not at all impossible that, in the future, such an understanding, resulting from the study of FOP, could lead to control over the process of bone growth.

< Sharks have provided researchers with some clues about bone development. Shark cartilage never develops into hard bones due to internal systems that restrict blood flow to the tissues.

Classification

CHAPTER 5

Morgellons Disease

Dr. Randy Wymore, an assistant professor of pharmacology and physiology at Oklahoma State University, peered through his microscope at fibers stuck to a slide. Packages containing these fibers had been arriving at his lab from all over the country, sent by people all claiming to have a similar skin ailment. In the past few weeks, Dr. Wymore had looked at hundreds of these fibers. They resembled nothing he had ever seen before—they were not hair fibers, skin or waste fibers, or textile material of any kind. Wymore assumed, however, that these fibers had to be something identifiable. He decided to contact the Tulsa Police Department. Since law enforcement

◁ A scientist prepares samples of fibers for analysis by a gas chromatograph. The sophisticated machine was unable to identify the source of fibers on the skin of Morgellons patients.

HEM\1\METHODS\

IZIA CRIMINALE
IZIA SCIENTIF
O-MERCEOLOGICE

43

organizations routinely identify fibers as part of criminal investigations, he thought the police might know what these fibers were.

A Mystery

Mark Boese and Ron Pogue, who have over 20 years of experience each as fiber experts, do critical crime lab analysis to help solve many kinds of crimes. While it had taken Dr. Wymore about nine months to be certain that the fibers were unusual, it took Boese and Pogue about three minutes.

Whatever the fibers were, they were far more exotic than lint. Tests were performed on the samples with a method of identification called gas chromatography. This involves

heating a sample in a vacuum until it melts and boils. The temperature at which this happens is specific to a particular compound, so it can be used to identify what the sample is made of. But when the machine had reached its highest temperature, 1,400 degrees, the fibers had only blackened slightly, neither melting nor boiling. In the end, the fiber experts were unable to identify the fibers. They did conclude, however, that the fibers were not man-made, nor were they from a plant.

Searching for Help

Although a huge question mark still surrounded the source of these fibers, Wymore's conclusion was a relief to Mary Leitao. Since 2002, she had been looking for someone to help her determine what was wrong with her then two-year-old son, Drew.

Drew had sores on his lip that would not heal, and he would point to the sores and complain of "bugs." Most unusual, there seemed to be bits of lint or fibers coming out of the sores. These fibers were often red, blue, black, or white. Leitao would brush them off and more would appear within days. Although she took her son to several doctors, including allergists, dermatologists, and pediatricians, no one was able

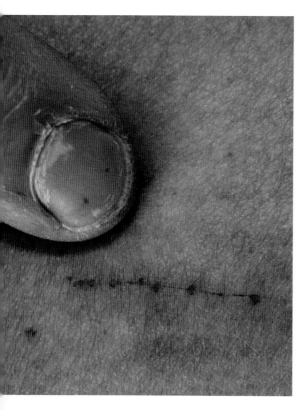

◁ A Morgellons sufferer points to an area on her skin from which the telltale fibers have emerged. People who claim to have Morgellons express the feeling that bugs are crawling on their skin in places where the fibers are found.

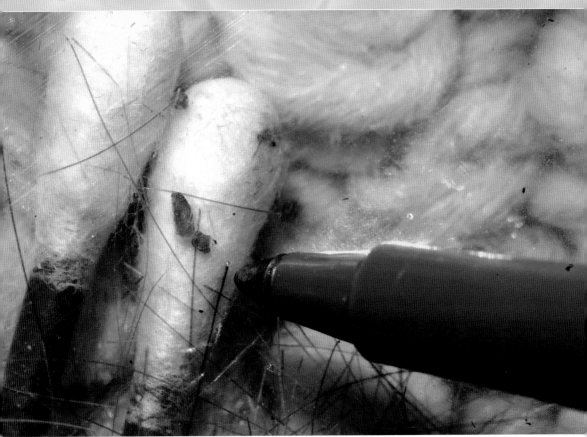

△ This enlargement of a cotton swab reveals particles that a Morgellons patient says emerge from her skin.

to identify the source of Drew's sores or the strange material creeping out of them. One well-known infectious disease specialist took one look at Drew's file and announced that it was Mary Leitao who was ill, that she suffered from Munchausen syndrome by proxy, a mental disorder that causes a parent to purposely sicken a child in order to seek attention from doctors.

Leitao, however, knew that her son was suffering from something real, and she was determined to find help. Spending hours on the Internet, researching any type of similar affliction, she came across a reference to something called Morgellons, a rare 17th-century sickness that involved hair or fibers growing from the body. Leitao started her own website to raise awareness of Drew's problems. Eventually, in March 2004, she started the Morgellons Research Foundation to raise money for scientific study of the disease. Almost immediately, people around the country began contacting her, complaining of symptoms that matched Drew's. Some of them also reported other symptoms, including difficulty concentrating, problems with short-term memory, vision loss, and depression.

A Growing Body of Evidence

Despite the continuing skepticism of most of the medical community, other evidence of Morgellons emerged. For one thing, the average Morgellons patient had no history of mental illness. There were also cases of young children whose sores were in places on their body that they could not have reached themselves. Other interesting facts have been discovered that may hold some keys to the disease. More than half of Morgellons sufferers also test positive for Lyme disease. Dr. Wymore and his colleagues have also found evidence of the fibers beneath unbroken skin in some patients. The Morgellons Foundation website has reported 2,000 cases of the disease as of February 2006.

In 2006, the Centers for Disease Control and Prevention (CDC), a government organization devoted to public health and research, acknowledged that Morgellons had become a public health concern. The CDC has decided to investigate. Its initial goal is to gather information about Morgellons—how it is contracted, whether it is contagious, what the risk factors are, and what symptoms properly identify the disease in individuals. The CDC team includes pathologists, toxicologists, mental health experts, infectious disease specialists, parasite experts, and environmental specialists.

In addition to Dr. Wymore's, other independent research efforts

∇ Verna Gallagher suffers from what she believes is Morgellons disease. It has left her debilitated and depressed. She is hoping the CDC will classify Morgellons as an actual disease and bring help to others with the affliction.

Skepticism and the Scientific Method

Scientists use a process called the scientific method to do their work. This involves observing and gathering evidence about a topic. Without evidence, there is no science. For the scientific method to work, scientists have to be skeptical. That means that they need to base their conclusions on the evidence, regardless of what they might believe or want to believe. When a new disease appears, doctors, who are essentially specialized scientists, must be skeptical about everything, even the existence of the disease itself.

Based on the evidence, a scientist then develops a hypothesis. A hypothesis is a reasonable "guess" that is based on evidence and can be tested by an experiment. After the experiment, scientists submit their results to other scientists, usually by writing an article that other scientists read. Scientists studying the same topic might repeat the original experiment to make sure the results are accurate. Then they might build on that previous work, or they might come up with an alternative hypothesis to account for the original experimental results. In that case, a new experiment must be designed to find out which hypothesis is correct.

When scientists come up with an idea that explains an observed phenomenon, they call it a theory. That means that, based on the current evidence, they think their idea is very likely to be true.

Scientists studying the bones of a skeleton make determinations about the individual based on a hypothesis that they will test to determine its certainty.

are ongoing. Some investigators are theorizing that the fibers are actually a fungus or even a never-before-seen parasite. Isolating and identifying the DNA of these fibers is the focus of most researchers, who believe that once the biology of the structures is determined, they can be compared to known agents of disease and perhaps treated with existing medications. Still other laboratories dispute earlier reports that these fibers are not plant-based.

The debate continues. Despite the lack of conclusive evidence, a growing number of scientists are convinced that while Morgellons has psychological side effects, the disease is definitely not all in the patients' heads.

Meet a Medical Researcher

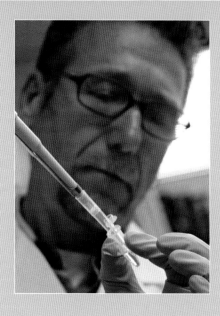

Dr. Randy Wymore is the director of the Center for the Investigation of Morgellons Disease at Oklahoma State University's Center for Health Sciences and an associate professor of pharmacology and physiology.

◨ How did you first become aware of Morgellons, and what made you decide to research it?

◨ In 2005 I did a literature and Internet search on the topic of "muscle fibers, diseases." I was trying to find a detail of information that a medical student had inquired about. One of the results that showed up on the search was entitled "the fiber disease." This led me to read several discussions about Morgellons disease and the unlikely symptom of lesions on the skin that are slow to heal and that seem to produce red, blue, clear, and black fibers,

sandlike granules, and black specks. Most dermatologists (skin doctors) across the U.S., Canada, and Europe were telling the people claiming to have Morgellons that there was nothing wrong with them; that they had no strange illness and the red and blue fibers were just tiny pieces of thread from their clothes, towels, or carpets. As a scientist, I thought it would be easy to test. Have a few people who claimed to have Morgellons send me fibers and then I could compare them with red and blue fibers from my own clothes. If the fibers were nylon or cotton, it should not be too hard to tell.

◨ At what point did you become convinced that Morgellons was a real disease?

◨ If scientists do an experiment, they usually need to have a hypothesis to test. My original working hypothesis was: "Morgellons fibers are nothing more than threads and fibers from the environment." Within a few days I had packages coming from California, Washington, Pennsylvania, Oklahoma, Florida, and Texas. They all contained samples of the supposed mysterious Morgellons fibers. The first thing I noticed was that these fibers did look similar to one another. The second thing I noticed was that the textile samples of threads did not really look anything like the Morgellons fibers. With textile fiber, there are often lines or imperfections when the synthetic textiles are made. With naturally occurring textiles (wool, llama wool, hair), it is usually easy to see the biological appearance of the fibers. I collected fibers from my clothes, my third grader's clothes, medical and graduate students' clothes, carpet fibers, towels, drapes, and even had several people collect dust bunnies from under their couches and furniture. None of these environmental fibers were quite like the Morgellons fibers. I was forced to reject my original hypothesis that Morgellons fibers were threads and environmental contaminants. Since I rejected the original hypothesis, I was left with the alternative: Morgellons fibers were associated with a previously unknown condition called Morgellons disease. At this point, I was greater than 90 percent positive that Morgellons disease was not an imaginary disease.

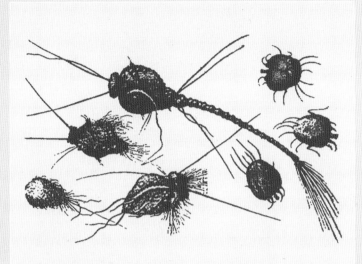

⚠ **A sketch from a 1687 scientist illustrates parasites found on the skin of children. They were described as looking like hairs. The Morgellons label originates from this condition although it is not certain that it is the same affliction.**

🔲 Why do you think so many people doubt Morgellons' existence?

🔲 Most people who consider themselves expert on a topic tend to be suspicious of something new that they have never heard of. This is especially so if the new thing sounds like something from a science fiction story. I thought the idea of red and blue fibers appearing in a person's skin sounded crazy at first. Now, after examining the supposed disease in some detail, I have changed my mind and am working to try to understand it.

🔲 What is your current research focusing on?

🔲 We are still trying to understand the chemical composition of the fibers. Chemists, biologists, and even geologists are assisting in trying to accomplish this. We are also isolating DNA from samples that doctors and others have sent to us. We use a molecular biology strategy that allows us to try to identify if there are any unusual bacteria, molds, or other organisms present.

🔲 Do you have any advice for people who might be interested in pursuing a career in medical research?

🔲 A scientist needs to be a person who is curious about the world. This is much like an explorer charting an unknown land. A person who is not curious about how things work will not typically become a scientist. A scientist also needs to learn the basic science tools that she or he will be using. Classes in math, chemistry, physics, and biology are the basics that a future medical researcher will need.

Physiology

CHAPTER 6

One Brain, Two Minds

Dr. Michael Gazzaniga, professor of psychology and the director of the SAGE Center for the Study of Mind at the University of California–Santa Barbara, is working with his patient, "Joe." Joe suffers from epilepsy and has undergone surgery to try to prevent the dreadful seizures he experiences. The results have been excellent, but Dr. Gazzaniga is not researching epilepsy. He shows Joe a computer screen with a dot in the center. As Joe stares at the dot, simple words and pictures appear either to the left of the dot or to the right of it. Joe identifies everything to the right of the dot, speaking the answers for the doctor. But he cannot seem to see what is going on to the

< A researcher studies parts of the human brain. Brain research yields more than just information about the mechanics of the body. Some scientists are studying how brain function determines personality and morality.

left of the dot. The screen shows a picture of a hammer to the right of the dot and a picture of a saw to the left. Joe sees only the hammer. But Joe is not blind in his left eye. Next, Dr. Gazzaniga puts a pen into Joe's left hand. He tells Joe to close his eyes and let his left hand draw whatever comes to mind on the paper in front of him. Joe draws a saw.

When Joe opens his eyes, Dr. Gazzaniga says it is a nice drawing. He asks what it is.

"A saw?" answers Joe.

"Yeah. What did you see?"

"A hammer."

"What did you draw a saw for?" asks Dr. Gazzaniga.

"I don't know," says Joe.

Λ Dr. Michael Gazzaniga's work with split-brain patients has resulted in a new understanding of how the human brain operates.

Learning from Surgery

You may have heard someone referred to as "left-brained" or "right-brained." This idea had its start in 1860 with the work of the German scientist Gustav Fechner. He theorized that if the human brain were divided in half, each half would have its own consciousness. Fechner's theory turned out to be correct.

Within your skull there are two separate versions of you. Each half of your brain, called a hemisphere, has its own awareness. This difference is not something you feel every day because the two halves are usually connected by a structure called a commissure. The commissure is made up of nerve fibers that allow messages to be sent back and forth between the two hemispheres.

But when the two halves of the brain become separated, as they do, for example, in a surgical procedure called a complete cerebral commissurotomy, it becomes astonishingly obvious how different they are. (A cerebral commissurotomy is performed on someone whose epilepsy is not responding to medication.) A damaged or modified brain is likely to cause severe medical problems in a patient—and sometimes death. Researchers cannot experiment on human brains, therefore, without an unacceptable risk to the patient. For this reason, a close observation of the effects of necessary surgery,

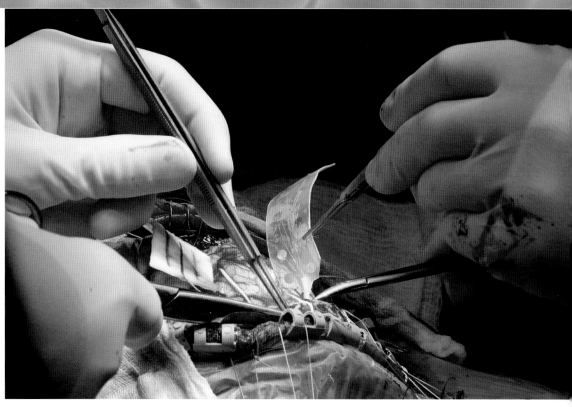

∧ **The brain of a two-year-old patient afflicted with seizures is operated on by neurosurgeons using material with sensors to determine the origin of the problem.**

or even accidents, was the only way to learn about the brain. It was not until commissurotomies were performed, beginning in 1961, that we found out how this amazing organ actually works.

Throughout the 1960s American neurologist Roger Sperry at the California Institute of Technology led a team in split-brain research. To learn how the halves of our brains relate to each other, Sperry's colleague, Michael Gazzaniga, headed up experiments researching and testing patients who had undergone this radical surgery. The results were startling, and they would later earn Sperry the Nobel Prize in medicine in 1981.

< **Brain research is moving in new directions at a rapid pace. One example of this is the development of a computer chip that can be implanted in the brain of paralyzed patients to allow them to send signals to a computer by just thinking about them.**

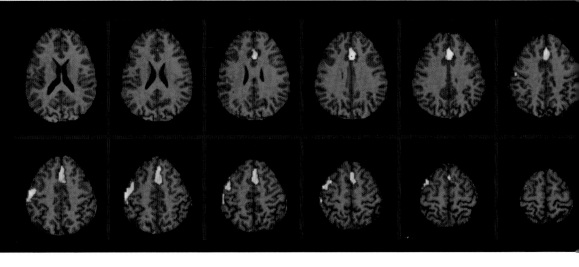

∧ Some researchers are looking into which parts of the brain are affected by different kinds of thinking. The results of an experiment on lying are pictured above. Certain areas of the brain show increased activity when a person lies.

Early Research

It was already known that each side of the brain tends to control the opposite side of the body. Your left brain controls your right hand, images from your left eye are understood by your right brain, and so on. Gazzaniga realized, however, that people rarely saw something with just one eye or were forced to touch something with just one hand. He suspected that the effects of having the two hemispheres of the brain separated probably went much deeper. His research team designed experiments to limit the information the body was receiving to just one half of itself, showing pictures to one eye only, for example.

The researchers would show an image—a picture of a boat, let's say—to a split-brain patient, but to the right eye only. When asked what she saw, she could say "boat"

Are You a Righty?

In scientific circles, some define handedness as whichever hand a person prefers to use. Others believe it is the hand that performs better on manual tests. Whichever the theory, most agree that a person is either left-handed or right-handed and it is these assumptions that have affected brain research since the mid-1800s. The French scientist Paul Broca first identified a region of the brain specialized for language and, at the same time, suggested that if a person were right-handed, he likely had left-brain dominance and vice versa. We know now that this doesn't hold true for all people. But until the mid-1960s when the Wada test was invented, research and surgery were based on this assumption. Handedness and its connection to either side of the brain remains mysterious, but many scientists believe that once we unlock the secret, we will have insight into a variety of language disorders, including dyslexia and stuttering.

since the left brain was "connected" to the right eye and also governed speech. When the same picture was viewed with the patient's left eye, she responded that she did not see anything. Even though the researcher was talking to both halves of the brain, only the left brain could answer! If the patient was asked to respond in a way that let the right brain answer nonverbally, by drawing a picture with the left hand, it became clear that the right brain was aware, but hidden from the left brain and unable to speak. When the patient was shown the boat through the left eye only and asked to draw what she saw, she could. But she had no idea why she chose to draw that particular object! The left brain did not know what the right brain saw.

▼ A machine measuring brain waves is used for researching epilepsy and sleep disturbance issues, and helps doctors with plans for brain surgery. Revolutionary tools like this one enable doctors to perform more brain operations than before because they provide the precision necessary for the task.

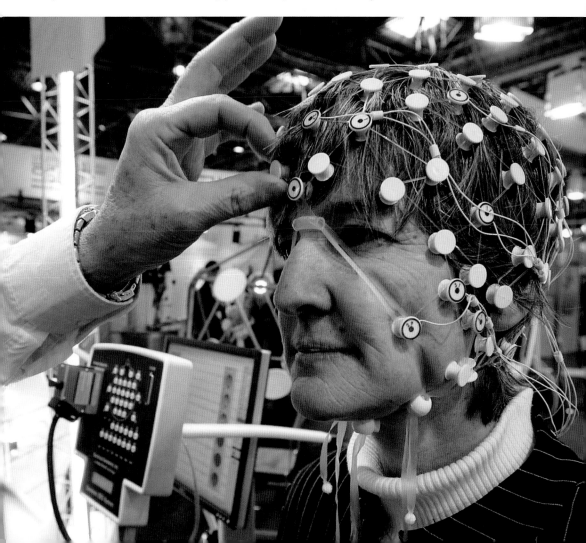

First, Do No Harm

Most of us trust doctors to do what is best for us, and so issues of right and wrong are most important. The study of right and wrong is called ethics. Medical ethics is what guides doctors to do the right thing. Most doctors guide their practice by the Latin phrase *primum non nocere*. It means, "First, do no harm."

In practical terms, this means scientists cannot experiment on people if such an experiment will do them harm. This is the dilemma that scientists who study how our brains work are up against. Instead of direct experimentation on humans, they must rely on careful observation of the effects of accidents and side effects of necessary surgery to provide the needed information.

Medical ethics are constantly evolving. One doctor, James Marion Sims, who worked in the 1800s researching women's medical issues, has come under scrutiny in the last decade. Much of his knowledge came from experiments performed on African-American slave women who did not give him permission. In late 2005, a

∧ James Marion Sims

committee of doctors voted to remove Dr. Sims' portrait from the wall at the University of Alabama because of his methods which, in the 1800s, were considered reasonable.

The high ethical standards of the modern medical community may be, in the end, that community's highest achievement.

Left- or Right-Brained

Gazzaniga and Sperry's experiments led to some general understandings of the hemispheres of the brain. The two halves of your brain are very specialized. Typically the left side of the brain deals with speech, language, and logic. The right half deals with how you think about spaces and shapes, how you picture things in your head, and music. There are exceptions, however.

Knowledge of the left and right halves of our brains is still imperfect at best. Language is one area doctors and scientists who perform and research split-brain operations pay particular attention to. Although language in 70 to 95 percent of human beings is controlled by the left half of the brain, for another 5 to 30 percent of the population, the same is not true. Before a split-brain operation can take place, doctors must perform a Wada test to find out which side of a patient's brain is responsible for language so extra care can be taken to avoid damage to that area. The Wada test is performed by injecting an anesthetic into the artery (a blood vessel that carries blood from the heart to other parts of the body) that supplies the blood to either the left or right side of the brain. It temporarily "puts to sleep" whichever side is targeted. When a patient is then asked to speak, doctors know if he cannot answer, the side of the brain that has been put to sleep is the dominant side responsible for language in that particular patient.

Dr. Gazzaniga is currently researching how some of his patients with damaged hemispheres or split brains have recovered their language and writing abilities. His research raises questions about how elastic the brain is and how it makes up for lost functions. New, high-tech methods of brain imaging are helping scientists map out how the two hemispheres receive and transmit information.

Most people think that "personality" has more to do with soul or spirit than with the brain's structure or physical function. But split-brain experiments suggest that one person's preference for math and figures over creative thinking could be a concrete result of the way the halves of his brain are wired together. More likely still, your personality could represent the compromise worked out between the two entities in your head regarding how best to solve the problems of everyday life.

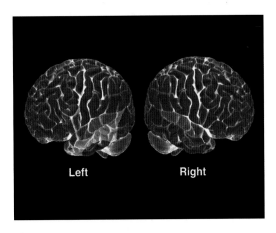

Left   Right

∧ The left side of the brain is typically responsible for speech, language, and logic, while the right side of the brain controls nonverbal functions like music and how we understand space and shapes.

Left Brain Functions	Right Brain Functions
Uses logic	Uses feeling
Detail oriented	"Big picture" oriented
Facts rule	Imagination rules
Words/language	Symbols/images
Present/past	Present/future
Math/science	Philosophy/religion
Can comprehend	Can "get it" (i.e. meaning)
Knowing	
Acknowledges order/ patterns	Believes
	Appreciates
Perception	Spatial perception
Knows object name	Knows object function
Reality based	Fantasy based
Forms strategies	Presents possibilities
Practical	Impetuous
Safe	Risk taking

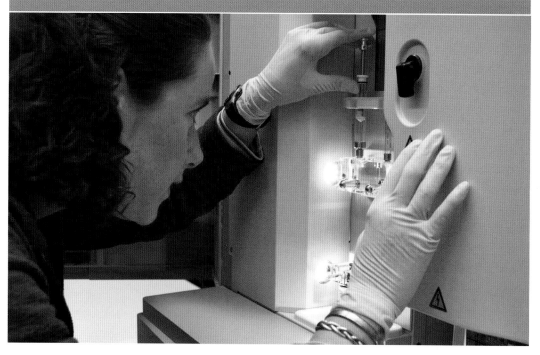

∧ A scientist monitors a DNA sequencing machine, a valuable tool in understanding the genes which make up the human body.

Science itself provides a good example of why the two halves of the brain need to work together successfully. Scientists use the systems of logic and data controlled by the left brain, but must also apply the larger ideas and concepts—and the flashes of insight—provided by the right brain. No scientist yet has determined which half of the brain gives rise to curiosity, which is often what keeps doctors and researchers on their path. In medicine, however, every answer has the potential to relieve suffering as well. If science is the quest to understand the world around us, medicine is the quest not only to cure but also to understand ourselves. Curiosity, technology, and painstaking research are the keys to unlocking the mysteries of the rare, bizarre diseases discussed in this book.

One valuable resource, the Human Genome Project, completed in 2003, provides doctors with a map identifying all of the more than 20,000 genes in the human body. This knowledge has already helped doctors like Kaplan and Shore, and will continue to give the medical community clues to understanding the diseases which plague humanity.

Great medical progress has been made in the past few years, encouraging those who suffer to look to the future with great hope.

Glossary

bacteria — single-celled organisms

cannibalism — the practice of eating parts of another person's body, usually for ritual or symbolic reasons

cell — a membrane-surrounded unit that is the basic structure of living things

chromosome — a threadlike strand of DNA in the cell nucleus upon which genes are located

epidemic — the rapid spread of a disease to many people

epilepsy — a disorder caused by abnormal brain nerve discharges

gene — the basic unit of inheritance of physical traits

hereditary — passed on to offspring from the parents

hypothesis — a proposed explanation for something that can be tested by an experiment

infection — invasion of the body or part of the body by dangerous microorganisms

ligament — cordlike tissue that connects muscle to bone

molecule — the smallest unit possible of a substance, composed of the minimum atoms necessary to make it up

muscle — tissue capable of contracting to produce movement in the body

mutation — an error in the genetic code, or the effect produced by such an error

paralysis — the condition of being unable to move

parasite — an organism that feeds off another organism, often living on or within it

scientific method — a formal system for the investigation of the physical world

skepticism — a deliberately doubtful attitude

symptom — a physical effect of a disease

theory — a hypothesis that accounts for a wide number of related phenomena

tissue — a group of cells in the body sharing a common function

trauma — sudden violent damage

virus — a microscopic infectious agent made up of genetic material surrounded by a protein shell, which hijacks healthy cells to make copies of itself

< Stem cells are the cells from which all the body's specialized cell types develop. Stem cell research may hold the answers to curing many of the diseases and ailments affecting people today.

Bibliography

Books

Benson, F. D., et al. *The Dual Brain (UCLA Forum in Medical Sciences).* New York: Guilford Press, 1985.

Gazzaniga, Michael. *Bisected Brain.* New York: Meredith, 1970.

Harris, D., ed. *Mad Cow Disease and Related Spongiform Encephalopathies.* Berlin Heidelberg: Springer-Verlag, 2004.

Mattson, M., et al. *Stem Cells: A Cellular Fountain of Youth.* Amsterdam, Netherlands: Elsevier Science B.V., 2002.

Prusiner, Stanley B., ed. *Prions Prions Prions (Current Topics in Microbiology and Immunology).* Berlin Heidelberg: Springer-Verlag, 1996.

Articles

BBC News. "Every Day Is a Bonus." August 6, 2004. http://news.bbc.co.uk/z/hi/health/3541836.stm (accessed March 28, 2008).

Collinge, J., et al. "Lessons from Kuru." *Lancet,* June 2006.

DeVita-Raeburn, Elizabeth. "The Morgellons Mystery." *Psychology Today,* March–April 2007. http://psychologytoday.com/articles/pto-20070227-000003.xml (accessed March 28, 2008).

Kaplan, Frederick. "Fibrodysplasia Ossificans Progressiva: An Historical Perspective." *Clinical Reviews in Bone and Mineral Metabolism 3,* no. 3–4 (2005): 179–181.

Maeder, Thomas. "A Few Hundred People Turned to Bone." *Atlantic Monthly,* February 1998. http://www.theatlantic.com/doc/19980z/bone (accessed March 28, 2008).

Quammen, David. "Deadly Contact." NATIONAL GEOGRAPHIC (October 2007): 78–105.

Reebs, S. "Cannibal Canard." *Natural History,* March 2006.

Seppa, Nathan. "Mad Cow Disease Might Linger Longer." *Science News,* July 15, 2006. http://www.sciencenews.org/articles/20060715/note11.asp (accessed March 28, 2008).

Weiss, Rick. "The Power to Divide." NATIONAL GEOGRAPHIC (July 2005): 3–27.

On the Web

Centers for Disease Control and Prevention **www.cdc.gov**

Creutzfeldt-Jakob Disease Foundation **www.cjdfoundation.org**

Genetics Home Reference **http://ghr.nlm.nih.gov**

International Fibrodysplasia Ossificans Progressiva Association **www.ifopa.org**

National Human Genome Research Institute **www.genome.gov**

Oklahoma State University Center for Health Sciences Morgellons Page **www.healthsciences.okstate.edu/morgellons/index.cfm**

Progeria Research Foundation **www.progeriaresearch.org**

Index

Boldface indicates illustrations.

Aging disease *see* Progeria
Alper, Tikvah 23
Alzheimer's disease 5

Bacteria 23, 24, 49, 59
Beef 26, **26,** 63
Berns, Sam 29–30, 33
Big toes, malformation of **34–35,**
    35, **38**
"blueprints," genetic 16, 29, 32
"Bodies...The Exhibition" (exhibi-
    tion) **18**
Boese, Mark 44
Bone growth, abnormal 35–41
Bovine spongiform encepha-
    lopathy (BSE) *see* Mad cow
    disease
Brain, cow's **25**
Brain, human
    early research 10, 54–55
    experiment on lying **54**
    funeral cannibalism 24
    hemispheres 10, 52–58, **57**
    measuring brain waves **55**
    physiology 18, 19, 51–57
    protein molecules 23
    split-brain patients 11, 51–52,
        54–55
Brain research **4,** 10, 11, **50–51,**
    51–57
Brain surgery 52–53, **53,** 54,
    55, 57
Broca, Paul 54

Cancer
    cells 16
    misdiagnosis 40
    research **16**
    treatment 33
Cannibalism
    definition 59
    Fore people 24, 27
Carl XVI Gustaf, King (Sweden)
    23
Cartilage 40, 41
Cells
    brain cell proteins 23
    cancer cells 16
    of children with progeria 29,
        31, **31,** 33
    computer model **27**
    definition 59
    stem cells 59
    see also Chromosomes
Centers for Disease Control and
    Prevention (CDC) 11, 46, 60

Chip, computer **53**
Chromosomes 16, **16,** 17, 32, 59
Circulatory system 18
Classification 17, 43–49
Collinge, John 21, 26–27
Collins, Francis 11, **30,** 31
Complete cerebral commissur-
    otomies 52
Computer modeling **27**
Cows
    brain **25**
    carcasses 25, **26**
    herd **11**
    mad cow disease 10, 11, 21,
        24–27
    protein supplements 25
    tissue samples **20–21**
Creutzfeldt-Jakob disease (CJD)
    5, 21–22, 25, 26–27
Crime lab analysis 44

Dermatologists 44, 48
DNA (deoxyribonucleic acid)
    32, 59
    double helix structure **10**
    errors 29, 31
    Morgellons research 47, 49
    samples **1**
    sequencing machine **58**
Drug treatments 33, 40
Dyslexia 54

Eastlack, Harry 35–37, **36**
    skeleton of **37**
Epidemics 11, 21, 27, 59
Epilepsy 51, 52, 55
Ethics, medical 56
    see also Hippocratic Oath
Europe: beef industry 26

Farnesyltransferase inhibitor
    (FTI) 31, 33
Fechner, Gustav 10, **10,** 52
Fibers, mysterious 43–44, **45,**
    46–49
Fibrodysplasia ossificans pro-
    gressiva (FOP) 10, 11, 17,
    35–41
Fore people 10, 24, 25, 26–27
Freke, John 10, 38
Funeral cannibalism 24
Fungi 24, 47

Gajdusek, Daniel Carleton 24
Gallagher, Verna **46**
Gas chromatography **42–43,** 44
Gazzaniga, Michael 51–52, **52,**
    53–57
Genes 16, **16,** 17, 32, 33, 41
    definition 59

number in human body 7, 58
    see also Human Genome
        Project
Genetics 16, 17, 29–33
Gordon, Leslie 31, **31,** 33

Handedness 54
Headaches 17, 24
Heart disease 30, 33
Heredity 17, 35–41
Hippocrates 19, **19**
Hippocratic Oath 19
Human body
    complexity 13–14, 15, 18, 22
    genes 7, 11, 58
    pathology 15
    physiology 18
    preserved specimens **18**
Human Genome Project 7, 11, 58
Hypotheses 47, 49, 59

Infections 15, 23, 26, 59
International Fibrodysplasia Os-
    sificans Progressiva Associa-
    tion (IFOPA) 40

Joints
    pain 24
    stiffness 30, 33

Kaplan, Frederick 11, 39, **39,**
    41, 58
Khan family **32**
Kos (island), Greece 19
Kuru 10, 23–24, 25, 27

Language 54, 56–57
Laughing death *see* Kuru
Left brain 52, 54–58
Left-handedness 54
Leitao, Drew 44–45
Leitao, Mary 44–45
Lesions 40, 48
Ligaments 38, 59
Logic 56, 57, 58
Longevity 33
Lying, experiment on 54, **54**
Lyme disease 46

Mad cow disease 10, 11, 21,
    24–27
McKusick, Victor 38
Meat processing plant **26**
Memory loss 23, 24
Molds 49
Molecules
    definition 59
    DNA 10, **10,** 32
    prions 23, 24
Morgellons disease 11, 17, 43–49

Morgellons Research Foundation 45, 46
Munchausen syndrome by proxy 45
Muscles 38, 59
Mutations, genetic 31, 33, 41, 59

National Institutes of Health 31
Nervous system 18, 23
New diseases 17, 26, 47
Nobel Prize winners 11, 23, **23,** 53
Norman family **17**

Papua New Guinea 10, 23–24
Paralysis 23, 24, 53, 59
Parasites 22, 24, 46, 47
    definition 59
    sketch **49**
Parkinson's disease 5
Pathogens 15
Pathologists **14,** 15, 21, 46
Pathology 14, 15, 21–27
Patin, Guy 10, 36, 38
Petri dishes **14**
Physiology 18, 51–57
Pogue, Ron 44
Prions **2–3,** 22–26
    discovery 11, 15, 22–23
    molecules 23, 24
    name meaning 22
    prion diseases 22, 23, 24, 26
    3-D model **22**
Progeria 11, 16, 29–33
Progeria Research Foundation (PRF) 30, 31, 33
Proteinaceous infections particles *see* Prions

Proteins 22, 23, 27, 33, 41, 59
Protozoa 24
Prusiner, Stanley B. 11, 22–23, **23**

Right brain 52, 54–58
Right-handedness 54

Scientific method 47, 59
Scrapie 22–23
Seizures 51, 53
Shark cartilage 40, 41
Sharks 40, **40**
Sheep **22,** 22–23, 25
Shore, Eileen 11, 39, **41,** 58
Sims, James Marion 56, **56**
Singh, Rajiv **27**
"Skeleton key" 39, 41
Skeletons
    physiology 18
    scientists studying **47**
    severely deformed **37**
Skepticism 47, 59
Skin
    color 17
    effects of progeria 20
    Morgellons disease 43–49
South Korea
    protest rally **63**
    U.S. beef imports 63
Speech 55, 56, 57
Sperry, Roger 11, 53, 56
Split-brain research 11, 51–57
Stem cell research **59**
Stomachaches 17
Stuttering 54
Surgery **12–13**
    see also Brain surgery

Tacket, John **30**
Textile fibers 43, 49
Theories, scientific 47, 52, 54, 59
Timeline of major medical mysteries 10–11
Tissue
    brain tissue 23
    definition 59
    samples **15, 20–21,** 23, 31
    sharks' tissues 40, 41
    see also Ligaments; Muscles
Traits, physical 17, 22, 59
Trauma 39, 59

United Kingdom
    cows **11,** 25
    mad cow disease 10, 11, 24–25, 27
    possible invisible epidemic 21, 27

Vaccine research **16**
Variant Creutzfeldt-Jakob disease (vCJD) 21–22, 26–27
Veterinarian **22**
Viruses 22, 23, 24, 59

Wada test 54, 56–57
Web sites 40, 45, 47, 60
Wymore, Randy 43–44, 46, **48,** 48–49

X-ray **34–35**
Xu, Meiqi **41**

Zasloff, Michael 38, 39, 40
Zoonosis 26

About the Author

A graduate of the University of Connecticut, Scott Auden has a lifelong love of exploring other cultures and meeting people from every possible background. In addition to teaching high school English, Auden has spent time teaching in the Japanese public school system, as well as teaching inmates inside maximum security prisons. His work as a freelance writer allows him to explore his love of learning with as broad a range of people as possible.

Auden is also the author of National Geographic's *Voices from Colonial America: New Hampshire.* He is married with two children.

About the Consultant

Dr. Elizabeth E. Brownell is a Family Practice physician. She is a 1988 graduate of St. George's University School of Medicine, Grenada, West Indies, and a 1991 Graduate of the Medical College of Wisconsin Family Practice Residency Program where she served as Chief Resident.

She served as Assistant Professor of Clinical Medicine, Medical College of Wisconsin from 1991-1994 and as Vice Chair of the Department of Family and Emergency Medicine at Waukesha Memorial Hospital, Wisconsin from 2000-2002.

Dr. Brownell has been in private practice since 1994 (including low-risk obstetrics until 2005). She resides in Merton, Wisconsin with her husband and two children.

V South Korean protesters rally against U.S. beef imports to their country amid scares of an outbreak of mad cow disease in 2006.

Founded in 1888, the National Geographic Society is one of the largest nonprofit scientific and educational organizations in the world. It reaches more than 285 million people worldwide each month through its official journal, *National Geographic,* and its four other magazines; the National Geographic Channel; television documentaries; radio programs; films; books; videos and DVDs; maps; and interactive media. National Geographic has funded more than 8,000 scientific research projects and supports an education program combating geographic illiteracy.

For more information, please call 1-800-NGS LINE (647-5463) or write to the following address:

National Geographic Society
1145 17th Street N.W., Washington, D.C.
20036-4688 U.S.A.

Visit us online at
www.nationalgeographic.com/books

For librarians and teachers:
www.ngchildrensbooks.com

More for kids from National Geographic:
kids.nationalgeographic.com

For information about special discounts for bulk purchases, please contact National Geographic Books Special Sales: ngspecsales@ngs.org

For rights or permissions inquiries, please contact National Geographic Books Subsidiary Rights: ngbookrights@ngs.org

Library of Congress Cataloging-in-Publication Data available upon request

Hardcover ISBN: 978-1-4263-0356-2
Library ISBN: 978-1-4263-0261-9

Printed in China

Book design by Dan Banks, Project Design Company

Published by the National Geographic Society

John M. Fahey, Jr., *President and Chief Executive Officer;* Gilbert M. Grosvenor, *Chairman of the Board;* Tim T. Kelly, *President, Global Media Group;* Nina D. Hoffman, *Executive Vice President; President, Book Publishing Group*

Prepared by the Book Division

Nancy Laties Feresten, *Vice President, Editor in Chief, Children's Books;*
Bea Jackson, *Director of Design and Illustrations, Children's Books;*
Amy Shields, *Executive Editor, Series, Children's Books*

Staff for This Book

Virginia Ann Koeth, *Editor*
Jim Hiscott, *Art Director*
Lori Epstein, *Illustrations Editor*
Lewis R. Bassford, *Production Manager*
Grace Hill, *Associate Managing Editor*
Jennifer A. Thornton, *Managing Editor*
R. Gary Colbert, *Production Director*
Susan Borke, *Legal and Business Affairs*

Manufacturing and Quality Management

Christopher A. Liedel, *Chief Financial Officer*
Phillip L. Schlosser, *Vice President*
Chris Brown, *Technical Director*
Nicole Elliott, *Manager*

Photo Credits

Front: Bobby Moodboard/Corbis
Back & Spine: Mehau Kulyk/Photo Researchers, Inc.
Back Icon: Shutterstock

AP = Associated Press; 1, Phanie/Photo Researchers, Inc; 2-3, Russell Kightley/Photo Researchers Inc.; 4, Simon Fraser/Newcastle General Hospital/Photo Researchers, Inc.; 6, AJ Photo/Photo Researchers, Inc.; 8, Courtesy of the consultant; 9 Photos.com; 10, Library of Congress; 10, Ben Greer/iStockphoto; 11 (top), U.S. Department of Energy Human Genome Program; 11 (bottom), AP; 12-13, Photos.com; 14 (top), Photos.com; 14 (bottom), 15, 16 (top), AP; 16 (bottom) Linda S. Nye/Phototake; 17, 18, AP; 19, New York Public Library; 20-21, Sean Gallup/Newsmakers; 22 (top and bottom), 23, 25 (top and bottom), 26, 27 (top and bottom), AP; 28-29, Courtesy of the Progeria Research Foundation; 30, AP; 31 (top) Keller and Keller, (bottom) Courtesy of the Progeria Research Foundation; 32, Deshakalyan Chowdhury/AFP/ Getty Images; 34-35, 36, 37, Courtesy of Frederick Kaplan and Joanne Deithorn; 38, IFOPA; 39, AP; 40, iStock; 41, Courtesy of Leslie Shore; 42-43, Mauro Fermariello/Photo Researchers, Inc.; 44, 45, 46, 47, AP; 48, 49, Courtesy of Oklahoma State University Center for Health Sciences; 50-51, SPL/ Photo Researchers, Inc; 52, Courtesy of Michael Gazzaniga; 53 (top and bottom), 54, 55, AP; 56, Library of Congress; 57, Zephyr/Photo Researchers, Inc.; 59, TEK Image/Science Photo Library; 63, AP

Front cover: Lab worker with petri dishes

Back cover: Microscope

Page 1: DNA samples stored at the French National Institute for Health and Medical Research are studied for genetic diseases.

Pages 2–3: An illustration of how prions might spread in the body. Normal prions are pictured as small green balls (center, right). Abnormal prions are a different shape (purple balls, upper right). Researchers are still unaware of how this abnormal protein gains a foothold on the body's cells.

A Creative Media Applications, Inc. Production
Editor: Susan Madoff
Copy Editor: Laurie Lieb
Design and Production: Luís Leon and Fabia Wargin